100 WAYS TO FLY MORE

100
WAYS TO
FLY MORE

AND GET MORE OUT OF FLYING

MATT FALCUS

First Edition 2017
ISBN 978-0-9955307-6-8

British Library Cataloguing-in-Publication Data
A catalogue record for this book is available from the British Library.

Published by Destinworld Publishing Ltd.
www.destinworld.com

© 2017 Matthew Falcus

Published by Destinworld Publishing Ltd.
www.destinworld.com
Interior design: Cover&Layout, www.coverandlayout.com

100 WAYS TO
FLY MORE

CONTENTS

INTRODUCTION

Whether you're an experienced pilot or a new pilot, the hard work of getting through your training and receiving the licence to fly is something that should not be taken lightly.

Too many pilots fall at the next hurdle, however, letting obstacles get in the way of building on that achievement and keeping their wings in regular use.

I am not writing this as a pilot who managed to escape this hurdle, but as one who fell into the trap and didn't make the most of being able to fly. Tempted to give it all up, I found it hard to fund flying more regularly than once per month, and when I did I ended up flying a well-worn trip around the local area as I had many times previously. My confidence to try new things or go places was low until I decided to do something about it. I've now managed to vastly increase my experience and the number of hours flown and, hopefully, become a better pilot as a result.

This book is written to encourage anyone with a private pilot's licence to get out there and find ways to fly more, and get more out of flying, through a hundred actionable tips. They are tips that I have put to use to get out of my own lack of flying, enabling me to enjoy the hobby so much more.

Split into themed sections, the 100 tips are aimed at pilots of all kinds of experience, from those who have just received their licence to those who have hundreds or thousands of hours of experience but are perhaps looking for a new challenge, or a way to keep up with it.

The tips are also there to encourage you to enhance your flying skills and gain valuable experience which you can only get from real-life flying, and which encourage safety to be upheld as a priority.

Regardless of your flying experience, I hope there will

be something in this book to encourage you to find ways to fly more and enjoy the wonders of controlling a complex machine high in the sky, enjoying the views and the places it will take you.

I'd like to thank all of those who have encouraged me in my flying over the years.

Matt Falcus

CHAPTER 1

ESSENTIALS FOR THE NEW PILOT

T he high of gaining your PPL is often followed by a sense of bewilderment. What do I do now? Where should I go? Can I just go and *fly*?

After the painful wait for your licence to arrive, which is a useful tool to prove you're not telling lies about becoming a pilot, the next steps often follow one of two paths…

First, new pilots often continue with what they know, hiring an aircraft from the club they had lessons with, and flying in the local area.

Second, pilots tend to drop away, not knowing how to advance further.

The tips in this section are aimed at brand new pilots looking for a bit of inspiration about what to do next and how to handle the responsibilities placed upon them.

1 FLYING IS YOUR RESPONSIBILITY

Whatever country you have learned to fly in, your new private pilot's licence comes with a range of requirements which are vital for you to keep on top of. These range from expiry dates of your licence to your pilot medical. If your local airport issues you an airside pass, it also may come with an expiry. And if you hire aircraft from a flying club, chances are they only consider you current if you've flown in the past month.

As a priority for being able to fly at all, you need to take responsibility for everything that comes with it. Make a plan to prepare in advance for expiries and know when you'll need to take biennial flight reviews, when your medical expires, and how long it has been since you last flew, so that you avoid disappointment.

2 SAFETY IS YOUR RESPONSIBILITY

If you're struggling for inspiration on where to fly or what to do once airborne, consider taking a refresher in an aspect of flying safely.

No pilot likes to think about having an in-flight emergency, but the reality is it can happen at any time to any pilot, no matter what their experience. So we all need to be familiar with how to deal with these situations.

Pick one situation at a time, or pick the one that you feel least confident in, and either take a flight with an instructor to safely practice the procedure, or walk yourself through the steps.

You should take time to do this regularly (your biennial flight review is a good opportunity) so that the response to any emergency becomes second nature to you. It may save your life.

3 TRY A DIFFERENT AIRCRAFT TYPE

Did you go through your whole training flying the same aircraft or aircraft type? After so many hours flying in this familiar machine, it can become comfortable to carry on taking it up every time you fly. However, part of the fun in being a pilot is in trying out different aircraft, and it is a useful step to take for a new pilot to challenge you a little.

New aircraft types need not be too taxing. For example, if you learned to fly in a Cessna 152, why not try a four-seat 172? Or a low-wing Piper type. These are fairly common at most airfields, and the differences are not too great. They can be covered with you in an hour or two by an instructor.

The benefits could see you now able to take more passengers flying, or being able to fly further.

Some aircraft types are a bit more complex, with different styles of control column or more advanced cockpit layouts. However, none are beyond your reach or capabilities now that you can fly.

4 SPEND SOME TIME FLYING ALONE

A lot of the fun of being able to fly is in taking people for a thrilling trip. Yet an important early step for any new pilot in gaining confidence and experience is to spend some time flying alone.

You will have done some of this whilst learning to fly, but you always had an instructor to call on as a backup and to help you plan your flying. Now, you are the pilot and the one responsible for planning your flights, ensuring the aircraft is safe to fly, and checking the weather is within limits.

Doing this repeatedly will give you confidence as a pilot, and will help you to make decisions for yourself in the air. You will start to form your own personal limits for flying.

5 PICK SOME PLACES YOU WANT TO GO OR SEE

Now that you don't have the restrictions of flying lesson requirements, you truly have the freedom to go and fly where you please. Many new pilots will fall into the trap of sticking within their comfort zones and flying in the local training area, or to an airfield that you've been to before. This can soon become boring, and many fall away from flying as a result.

Therefore, as an early experiment to keep you flying more, make a list of the places you want to go and the places you want to see from the air as an inspiration for pushing yourself further.

When I gained my licence I decided I wanted to try out some photography of landmarks and towns in my part of the world, so I set about planning routes that would take in these attractions. People loved to see the pictures back home, which gave me an extra buzz to go out and do more.

6 CONNECT WITH AND LEARN FROM OTHER FLYERS

Flying is a very popular hobby the world over, and you are now a part of this global community. You may have made some friends among the people at your flying club, but there are thousands more out there to connect with and learn from.

Popular online communities on Facebook and web forums are a place where pilots and students post questions, ask advice, show off photos from their latest trip, or even their new aircraft and equipment purchases. This is the perfect way to gain knowledge and tips on how other pilots just like you are spending their time.

Most members are eager to help out new pilots and offer advice and encouragement, and you may even find yourself invited to a fly-in or to tag along as a second pilot on a trip.

Circling over Durham Cathedral. Aerial sightseeing is a great reason to pick new routes to fly.

7 SET YOURSELF SOME FLYING TARGETS

A common factor in pilots not getting airborne as often as they had hoped is in restrictions on time and finances. It's important to be realistic about what you'll be able to achieve, and to ask yourself what you want to do with your pilot's licence.

Are you working towards a career as a pilot? Are you hoping to become an instructor? Or, like most people, do you just want to do this for fun?

Once you've decided this, think about your finances and how much money and time you can commit to pursuing flying without it becoming a burden.

With all of this in mind, make a plan for how many hours you're going to fly this year; what extra ratings you want to train for; which airfields you want to fly to. Budget for these and plan ahead, and you'll make sure you fly more this year.

8 HANG AROUND THE FLYING CLUB AND PICK UP IDEAS

Chances are that on a rainy or windy day you won't be the only one moping around the airfield, eagerly refreshing the weather forecast. If you fly from a club there will probably be other pilots and instructors hanging around with nowhere to go too.

Grab a coffee and have a conversation about your latest flying, and pick the brains of others who may have flown to an interesting place, or even had an emergency to deal with lately. It can be great for new pilots to have this inspiration, or to get some refresher tips, and you may even find a buddy for a future flight.

CHAPTER 2

TRY FLYING FURTHER

So you've managed to keep in the habit of flying after gaining your licence. When you dreamed of becoming a pilot, did you always want to be able to go exploring and visit new places?

In this section we look at some ideas of how to take a plane away from the comfort of your home airfield and get into the habit of flying to other airfields and sightseeing from the air.

Once you get started with this it becomes less difficult to make sense of the process of getting from A to B.

1 PICK A NEW AIRFIELD

As I mentioned earlier, one of the factors that causes pilots to fall away from flying is boredom with doing the same thing every time they fly.

A great way to add variety and add a challenge is in flying somewhere new. There are hundreds of airfields and airports open to light aircraft, both near and far. And there are good guides produced by AFE and Pooleys which provide maps and instructions on how to fly to each one, from the smallest grass strip to large airports.

A good first step is to pick an airfield within an hour's flying time from your home base which is not too difficult (especially if you are not used to grass strips or short runways, for example). Read up about it, find out about their landing fees and whether you need permission to fly there, look up any videos on YouTube or trip reports on pilot websites, and then plan your route.

Go over it a few times beforehand, and especially on the day you fly, so that it is committed to memory. Plan the radio frequencies you'll need to speak to and check the weather at the destination and along the route. Call the airfield for permission and to ask if there are any important instructions for landing there.

Every airfield has its own community of flyers and they welcome visiting pilots. Once you land you'll be welcomed into this community, and you'll feel the buzz of having used your license to fly somewhere new. What's more, you'll want to go and do it again!

2 PICK AN AIRFIELD OVER 150 MILES AWAY

Having gotten used to flying to other airfields, a good next step is to fly somewhere even further away. The process of doing so is no different from a planning perspective, but it will give you more experience in navigating a longer route. No doubt you will also speak to more radio frequencies along the way.

It's interesting to see how far you can travel by air in so little time compared to car travel. Reaching another part of the country is easy and quick, making day trips or weekends away possible if you have access to an aircraft for longer periods.

3 FIND ANOTHER PILOT TO FLY TO OTHER AIRFIELDS WITH

Flying long distances on your own can sometimes be a little intimidating, especially for newer pilots who don't have much experience. It can also be expensive to do often and, let's face it, lonely at times.

Buddying up with another pilot is a great way to combat this. You'll have an extra pair of hands for flying (consider dividing up responsibilities, such as flying and radio communication), an extra set of eyes out of the window, someone to run questions by if you are unsure of anything, and someone who you can share the costs with. Then, once you've landed, you have a friend to enjoy that coffee and bacon sandwich with in the club café!

Having a pilot buddy to fly with is a great confidence builder and an encouragement to get out and fly more.

4 GET HOLD OF NAVIGATION SOFTWARE

Over the past few years technology has caught up with general aviation in a big way. Where pilots of days gone by had to rely on archaic methods of navigating and planning routes, today we have a range of apps for tablets and smart phones which can do all of the work for you and present it in a visually appealing way.

I'm not saying you should forget about how to read a map and plan a route by hand, as you the threat of technology failing is always a possibility. Those skills are imperative for any pilot to be able to fall back on.

However, investing in apps which can plan routes, show live weather, danger areas, NOTAMs and your current position, as well as those which help you plan weight and balance and provide the correct aircraft checklist offer a major reduction in pilot workload.

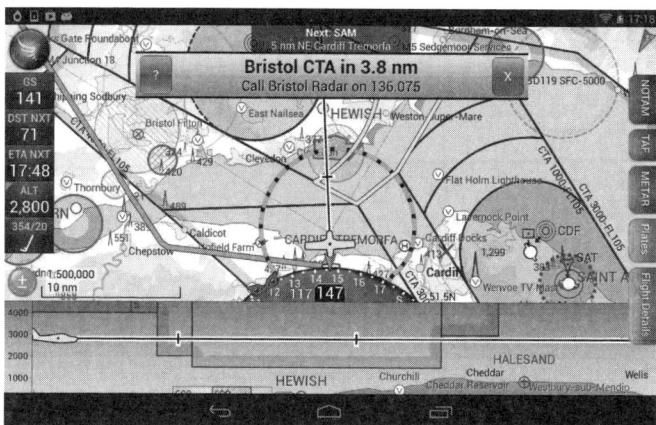

SkyDemon has made navigating in the air and planning routes so much easier.

Since starting to use SkyDemon navigation software, I now find myself planning and flying so many more trips than I did previously.

5 FLY TO A GRASS AIRFIELD FOR THE FIRST TIME

If you were lucky enough to learn to fly on a grass runway you may wish to skip ahead on this one. For me, having learnt to fly on a 2,200m long concrete runway, the prospect of using grass strips was alien and a little frightening at first.

However, after gaining my PPL I employed my flying instructor in taking me through some practical training. We covered the theory and flew to three different local grass airfields, each with different kinds of challenges, such as runway length, runway slope, nearby obstacles and overhead join procedures. This was a great help in giving me the confidence to start using these smaller airfields, with their different R/T communications (or none at all) and runways that seemed to run out after no time!

If you've only been flying from the safety of larger controlled airports with long runways, learning to use smaller grass strips will open up a new world of opportunities for you to fly more.

6 FLY INTO A BUSY AIRPORT FOR THE FIRST TIME

Now, the opposite goes for those who are only used to the freedom of small airfields with grass strips, relaxed radio communications and a club atmosphere. Flying into a larger, busy airport requires everything to be done by the book. Often there is controlled airspace to operate in, and air traffic control will work to fit you in to a busy pattern of aircraft up to airliner size. Then, on the ground there are instructions on which taxiways to use, where to park, and even gaining permission to start your engine again.

The two types of airfield are a world apart. Using busy airports requires concentration and discipline to work safely with ATC instructions. But once you've done it you have a world of new opportunities of places to fly.

Whilst many large international airports don't allow light aircraft (or charge the earth for landing fees), there are plenty who thrive on this kind of traffic and are very welcoming.

7 PLAN A CROSS-COUNTRY TRIP THROUGH DIFFERENT KINDS OF AIRSPACE

Regardless of whether you learned to fly at a small airfield or larger airport, you will be used to the airspace around this airfield. Perhaps it is controlled airspace, or maybe Class G airspace where you have the freedom of the skies.

Now, look at a map of the airspace across the country. Imagine a route to another airfield and think about whether you'd fly in a circuitous pattern through open airspace to get there, or whether you'd try to fly through the different control zones along the route.

The latter is more intimidating, but is the preferred option given it will save you time; it will also give you experience in dealing with different air traffic centres who will vector you and give you permission through their airspace (or ask you to stay outside, which is fine too). Avoiding airspace because it seems easier will not make you a better pilot, so plan a route to get the experience in different kinds of airspace.

8 INVESTIGATE AIRFIELD BREAKFASTS

You've probably heard of the $100 hamburger. It's a popular phrase used by American pilots for their love of taking a flight to another airfield for lunch. This connection between food and flying seems common the world over, but here in the UK seems to revolve more around a good breakfast.

Airfield cafes across the country do a swift trade in bacon sandwiches, or all-day breakfasts, and whenever I talk to pilots about where they've been flying lately the conversation usually revolves more around the quality of the food than the quality of the runway.

If you're interested in rewarding your ever-increasing confidence in flying to other airfields, why not do some research into the best breakfasts available, or even start offering your own ratings to other pilots.

9 GO AERIAL SIGHTSEEING

I've mentioned this before. When I first gained my licence and started flying for fun, one of the first things I did was take the camera with me and start flying over local landmarks and interesting places. People loved seeing the pictures afterwards, and I started discovering a love for the landscape around me as it always seemed to throw up new and interesting places when seen from above.

I soon discovered that different weather conditions and times of the year also changed how this scenery looked, adding a new dimension to sightseeing.

The places you can fly to across the country have all manner of local landmarks to see from the air, so plan these into your routes too!

CHAPTER 3

TRY SOMETHING
MORE CHALLENGING

t's important to keep growing your skillset if you are to make the most out of being a pilot. It helps you to stay safe, and it pushes you to experience new ways of flying.

From gaining extra ratings to flying further afield, there are many options for trying something more challenging. Which you choose will depend on your finances, your confidence, and how far you want to go as a pilot.

Not all of these tips are essential, but a guide to what can be achieved if you pursue a certain direction.

1 LEARN TO FLY A TAILWHEEL AIRCRAFT

Once upon a time tailwheel aircraft were all anybody flew, so it was perfectly normal to take flying lessons and gain your licence with your nose pointed to the sky when sat on the ground. Today, however, tailwheel aircraft are few and far between in most parts of the world, and seen as something of a novelty for a pilot to fly.

It is unlikely that a tailwheel, or "taildragger" is ever going to be a requirement of your flying (it's only in the bush, such as in Alaska, where these types are useful for landing on unprepared strips, for example), but flying one is something to experience. Doing so will hone your flying skills just a little bit more, changing the perspective from nose-up flare to a more nose-down flare, and taxying around the airfield looking out of the side of the cockpit to see where you're going.

Plenty of specialist clubs offer tailwheel conversions, adding an endorsement to your licence to go off and fly these often historic aircraft types. It usually takes up to ten hours of training to get signed off, and I recommend doing so as there are many nuances to transitioning and times when the newbie can get a little tangled up in controlling the plane on the ground.

2 INCREASE THE NUMBER OF FIELDS VISITED IN A WEEKEND

Here's a challenge to set yourself: try to visit an increasing number of airfields on a single day. I appreciate your home location may not offer too many choices within range, but try it out.

Get hold of your maps and airfield guide book and plan to add one more (or one new) airfield to a trip each time you go out flying on a weekend. This works really well in the summer months when you have sunshine and lots of light to play with, not to mention dry ground.

You could pick one long leg followed by a series local airfields, or you could set yourself a circuitous route around the country taking in places you've never been to before.

3 COMMIT TO LEAVING THE SAFETY OF YOUR LOCAL AREA

There's always a temptation when you want to go flying but have no firm plans, to just stick with what you know. That is, to fly from the airfield you always fly from, and potter about in the immediate area which you know so well. You probably did your training here. You have probably taken all of your friends and family on flights around here. You see the same landmarks and towns as you always do. And it is no challenge or fun any longer.

This is a waste of money and a waste of the licence you worked so hard to gain. So, with a bit of forethought, every flight you take this year can be something new, something challenging, or something that takes you to a place you've always wanted to go.

By doing so your confidence in flying and navigating will grow immeasurably and you'll finally have the stories to tell people of the places you've been able to visit as a pilot.

4 TRY OUT SOARING IN A GLIDER

To gain a true respect for the mechanics and beauty of flight, soaring in a glider cannot be beaten. Many pilots wrongfully assume that glider flying is the easier, simpler relation to powered flight. This, however, is not the case as gliding requires a sound understanding of all the same principles of flight, but with the added pressure of using the air and thermals to remain in flight; it's adding an engine which makes things simple.

The glider aircraft itself is very basic, with few instruments to worry about. Before flying, the external walkaround has much fewer points of interest given the lack of engine, fuel and oil. But let's not belittle these amazing aircraft – they can fly at 90kts, up to 20,000ft, and cover distances of hundreds of miles.

Anyone mastering the skills of gliding needs to have a good understanding of the effects of weather, and how the aircraft can harness energy to remain in flight and even travel long distances.

Glider clubs can usually be found along ridgelines in any country, and soaring is becoming increasingly popular among both new and experienced pilots alike.

5 MAKE EACH TRIP LONGER THAN THE LAST

A great way to build up confidence in cross country flying is to push your limits a little further each time you fly. For example, if you flew a half-hour trip to another airfield last time, why not push for somewhere an hour away next time? Or if you visited a benign flat grass runway on your last flight, why not pick something more challenging next time, like a runway on a hill?

By doing this regularly you'll not only find your trips more interesting, but your skills will also increase in handling the aircraft in different situations. You will also become more comfortable communicating to different types of services along the way.

By building up the length of your trips, soon you'll find yourself exploring destinations much further from home, or even other countries.

6 FLY IN A SSDR AIRCRAFT

The latest craze in light aircraft is the Single Seat Deregulated, or SSDR, which has opened up a new world of affordability and flexibility for recreational pilots.

SSDRs are, as the name suggests, single-seat aeroplanes. They fall under the microlight category, which are sub-300kg, and only require pilots to have the basic national pilot's licence to fly (if you already have a PPL, you only need a simple check flight with a microlight instructor to cover the differences).

SSDRs in the USA are known as Light Sport aircraft, and are just as popular there. The main draws are the fact that these aircraft usually look like regular aeroplanes, but are significantly cheaper to operate and maintain. You can enjoy flying for a fraction of the cost, often with modern avionics on board.

The drawback is that you're on your own up there; no taking the family touring or a friend for a spin above the local countryside. You're also limited by the weight you can carry, and the weather you can fly in.

However, single-seat or light sport aircraft are a very affordable way into aircraft ownership.

7 ATTEND A GENERAL AVIATION TRADE SHOW

Shows are organised all over the world for light aircraft pilots which allow manufacturers to showcase their latest products to potential buyers. The stars are usually the latest aircraft, and recently this has been SSDR/Light Sport aircraft (see previous tip on this). However, you can also top up on everything you need, from books to oil, camera attachments to flying suits. At most of the events I have attended, seminar sessions are also held covering the latest tips and inspiration for pilots, and updating them on new regulations and safety issues. It can leave you planning something more challenging with your flying, having gained some insight at the show.

In the UK there are two main trade shows at present – Aero Expo, usually held in June, and FLYER Live, usually held in December. Elsewhere you may want to try Aero Expo Friedrichshafen (April), Sun 'n' Fun in Florida (April), or EAA AirVenture at Oshkosh, Wisconsin (July).

8 TRY AIR RACING

The Royal Aero Club states that "air racing… is certainly

Single Seat Deregulated aircraft are an affordable way into flying and aircraft ownership.

as old as aviation itself". It is a natural draw for the more adventurous, competitive types of pilots, who compete for trophies in speed and navigation every year. Maybe you'd like to get involved too?

Pilots involved in air racing tend to become part of a 'scene', where race events turn into social occasions which are great fun.

Surprisingly, air racing is not that hard to get into. The aforementioned Royal Aero Club (www.royalaeroclubrrra.co.uk) requires pilots have 100 hours of pilot-in-command time, and a form signed by a Certified Flight Instructor. You then pay your entry fee and can take part. Naturally you need access to an aircraft capable of at least 100mph in level flight.

It's normal that for each race you are checked out and instructed around the circuit first. Your skills will be honed the more you race, and newbies have been known to win!

CHAPTER 4

AIRCRAFT OWNERSHIP

Owning an aircraft is the ultimate goal for many new pilots who want to shake off the shackles of the flying club and truly explore their wings.

To get into aircraft ownership the pilot needs to grasp the complicated process. Unlike buying a new car, pilots will often buy aircraft which are sometimes decades old. They need to fully check and understand the paperwork and the aircraft's maintenance history, as well as registering the aircraft with the aviation authority.

There are cheaper ways to go about aircraft ownership, as we'll explore, leading you to greater freedom and some much more affordable per-hour flight costs.

1 FIND WHO OWNS AIRCRAFT AT YOUR NEARBY AIRFIELD

If you're new to the whole concept of owning aircraft and everything that comes with it, it would be a good idea to speak to others who have gone there before you.

First off, it's a great way to meet fellow flyers around your local airfield. Secondly, you'll be able to pick their brains about the costs and other requirements; not just in the aeroplane itself, but in hangarage and airport fees, and what pitfalls they've come across.

This could open a door to buying a share in a plane, or in sourcing an aircraft that might be for sale.

2 BUY A SHARE IN AN AEROPLANE

If you have ambitions to own your own aeroplane now that you have that coveted pilot's licence, often the best way to start is by purchasing a share in an aircraft with other people. A share operates whereby a group of (often around ten) pilots share the ownership and costs of an aircraft, and benefit from being able to fly it whenever they wish. This saves a number of headaches, especially if you've never owned an aircraft before.

First, it allows you to try out ownership without suffering the full financial cost of buying an aeroplane. Buying a share will cost a fraction of the full price, and you can sell that share if or when you decide to.

Secondly, you'll get the knowledge of the rest of the group. This is particularly useful when it comes to aircraft maintenance, insurance, registration and paying airport fees.

Finally, owning a share of an aircraft gives you the ability to fly at much cheaper rates than if you are hiring an aircraft from a flying club, and the freedom to take it away for extended periods, such as a weekend trip.

Owning a share is a fantastic way to fly more and to explore the possibilities of aircraft ownership, but make sure you can afford the monthly costs and plan to fly enough to justify it.

3 BUY YOUR FIRST AEROPLANE

If you have the means to do so, the best way to have the freedom and encouragement to fly more is by owning your own aeroplane.

With it available whenever you want it, going flying is easy and convenient, and you are in complete control of the costs involved without paying premiums for hiring aircraft.

Ownership comes with the burden of maintaining, insuring and paying all of the fees involved in keeping it at an airfield. The initial outlay is also a major stumbling block for some pilots, although specialist lenders can help make the dream a reality.

Once you have experienced it, your flying will literally take off with the possibilities of flying holidays and taking the family on extended trips whenever you feel like it.

4 KNOW THE COSTS UP FRONT

When buying an aeroplane, it can be very easy to be caught up in the excitement of it. Like buying a sports car, it's easier to imagine yourself enjoying the powerful engine, cockpit gadgets and entertaining friends on trips. However, buying something that fits within your needs is a wiser choice, and it's important to know up front what costs you are likely to meet.

For example, an aircraft may appear affordable but its engine might soon be due an overhaul. Investigate this, and the cost you will be faced for that overhaul. Similarly, look for any problems with the airframe, interior and avionics for signs that a replacement or repair will be due.

Consider also the availability of parts and places which are capable of overhauling this type of aircraft. Simple, common aircraft are much easier and cheaper to service than a more complex type where the only service centre is in another country.

CHAPTER 5

ADDITIONAL LICENCES AND EXPERIENCE

The basic private pilot's licence is all any of us needs in order to be allowed to fly, and you may be happy with that.

Adding new ratings and licences is a natural progression towards becoming a commercial pilot, and are often taken in a modular fashion.

If you intend to always be a recreational pilot, these additions are not necessary at all. However, they can add a layer of safety to your flying, and give you more scope and flexibility should weather conditions prove a problem. And some are just plain fun!

1 GET A NIGHT RATING

In the UK and many other countries, particularly in Europe, a PPL licence does not come with a night flying endorsement, so if you're reading this in the USA you can skip ahead.

Many pilots will add a night rating during their training, or complete it shortly after gaining their licence. It is the easiest rating to add, and opens up more flying hours, particularly in countries where the darkness of winter severely restricts flying.

Having this rating means you will no longer risk being stuck away from home if the sun sets before you're able to return.

It also opens up a world of incredible views of the cities, towns and landscape around you as you've never seen them before.

2 GET AN IMC OR EIR RATING

The basic private pilot's licence gives you the skills to fly when the weather and visibility is good enough to avoid risking your safety. However, pilots flying in countries such as the United Kingdom and Ireland where marginal weather occurs more often than not can find it incredibly frustrating to deal with the limitations imposed on them.

A 'get out of jail card' has been available for many years in the form of the IMC rating (or Instrument Rating (Restricted) rating), issued by the UK Civil Aviation Authority. It allows pilots to fly in instrument meteorological conditions (IMC), such as reduced Special VFR inside controlled airspace, VFR conditions above clouds, and even to make instrument landings in Class D airspace.

The IMC rating is not a full IFR rating, and the training is limited in comparison. However, it is an added level of safety and training on flying by instruments should you ever find yourself in worsening weather conditions whilst aloft.

It should be noted that the CAA intends to stop issuing the IMC rating from April 2019. In its place is the En Route Instrument Rating (EIR) which offers the same privileges without the ability to perform instrument approaches or commence a flight in IFR conditions.

3 GET A FULL INSTRUMENT RATING

More than just a 'get out of jail free' card, the full Instrument Rating is for those serious about flying, either as a future career or as something you will want or need to be doing in all weather conditions and in airways used by commercial aircraft.

It is, therefore, more expensive and onerous to undertake the full rating, but a great weapon in your arsenal of flying skills. You also need a Class 1 Medical.

Many flying schools offer the Instrument Rating course, which comprises 50 hours of training for a single-engine aircraft, plus exams.

An alternative to the full Instrument Rating is a new option known as the Competency Based Instrument Rating, or CBM IR. It requires you to demonstrate your instrument flying skills without the depth of theory knowledge and training time. You will need 50 hours of cross-country pilot-in-command experience and a Class 2 Medical with extra hearing test to start training, and undertake 40 hours of instruction.

These days instrument training can be partly conducted on approved simulators, which many flying schools now boast as part of their setup. This naturally reduces training costs.

4 GET AN INSTRUCTOR RATING

Have you ever considered using your piloting skills to teach new pilots? Becoming a flying instructor is a great way to pass on your love of flying and help others in their quest to become a pilot. Flying instructors also generally fly a lot more than your average pilot.

To be awarded a flying instructor rating (FI), you need to have completed 150 hours of pilot in command time and have flown a route of 300nm taking in at least two other airfields. Then, completing a course of practical and ground school training, you'll obtain the ability to teach and earn money from flying. No longer do you need to gain a commercial pilot licence in order to teach and earn money as a flying instructor, however you'll need to complete a couple of the commercial exams to teach the full licence.

Once you sign up with a flying school you'll be flying all of the time, taking students through the syllabus, and also taking lots of taster flights. This is a great way to build hours and experience if you're working towards an airline job.

5 GET A MULTI-ENGINE RATING

If you have ambitions to take your flying along the commercial route, a natural early steps is in transitioning to aircraft with more than one engine. This complex training is undertaken by flying schools which specialise in commercial pilots, giving you a Multi-Engine Rating.

Few pilots will then use this as a means of recreational flying, but as a stepping stone towards a commercial rating either on turboprop or jet engine aircraft.

6 GET A SEAPLANE RATING

Like tailwheel flying, seaplane aircraft are not all that common as they tend to be used only in areas where light aircraft are a way of getting around, or as a tourist attraction. Think Alaska, northern Canada, the Maldives etc. Therefore, you may never have the need to get a seaplane rating, but it's often seen as one of the most fun things you can do as a pilot.

Again, like the tailwheel conversion, once in the air there isn't much difference to flying the plane. The tricky part comes in the take-offs, landings and navigating around the airfield (or seaport in this case), and it can be a difficult thing to master.

Unlike taxying around an airfield on the ground, doing so in a seaplane around an open stretch of water does not come with the advantage of brakes, and the aircraft is at the mercy of the wind and water currents, making docking very difficult to master. A whole host of other factors come into play when landing and taking off, such as wave size and other marine traffic getting in the way; there's rarely a defined landing strip being kept clear by ATC!

It usually take 7-10 hours of training and a skills test (which is valid for a year) to gain a seaplane rating in the UK. In the USA there is no test, only an endorsement from a Chief Flying Instructor once you've taken some training.

7 BECOME A GLIDER PILOT

Gaining a glider pilot licence can be done as either a first step into flying, or as an addition to your existing full pilot's licence. For a new pilot, gliding is a less expensive way to fly and requires less in the way of written exams, although a full EASA Part FCL licence and medical will be required from April 2018. You can also credit 10 percent of your gliding time towards your private pilot training (up to a maximum of ten hours).

For the experienced pilot, gaining a gliding endorsement on your licence simply requires experience from a gliding club and a form to be filled out.

Many clubs offer complete training and conversion training, and are happy to discuss this with you or take you on a trial flight.

8 BECOME AN AEROBATIC PILOT

There are few better ways to really get to grips with flying an aeroplane than through aerobatic flying. The accurate, positive and intense controls required are an excellent way to expand your abilities as a pilot, and it's open to any PPL to try.

It's important to stress that performing aerobatic manoeuvres should not be attempted without an instructor, or in an aircraft not certified to handle them.

Before beginning aerobatic flying it would be prudent to take an experience flight first to understand just how different it is, both in terms of flying, and in terms of the stresses put on the body. It's not uncommon to feel nausea and extreme G forces on the body which can be unpleasant. If you know an aerobatic pilot, ask them to take you for a flight to try it out.

Your next step should be to find a training organisation which offers aerobatic licences. In Europe the EASA Aerobatic Rating (AR) and the AOPA Basic Aerobatic Certificate are a good introduction and should see you being certified in a minimum of eight hours. Standard and Intermediate certificates can also be undertaken depending on experience and how far you want to take your aerobatic flying.

CHAPTER 6

FLYING WITH OTHERS

N ow that you're no longer stuck with an instructor in the right-hand seat bearing down on you and criticising your every move, you have a space (or spaces) to fill in the aircraft.

If you're a new pilot, no doubt you'll be itching to show off your ability to fly to your friends and family. From a spin about the local area to taking people on an extended trip or holiday, the opportunities are endless.

1 TELL YOUR FRIENDS AND FAMILY THAT YOU CAN FLY!

I'm sure this won't need too much encouragement for anyone who is thrilled at the fact that they have just earned a private pilot's licence through hard work and determination. You can fly! You can also now take people flying, which is a thrilling experience.

Tell your friends and family that you have a pilot's licence and you'll have a line of people waiting for the opportunity to come fly with you. What more encouragement do you need to get out there any fly more?

2 TAKE A FAMILY MEMBER FLYING

The first step is naturally to take a family member or close friend flying.

Think about your local area and the sights you can see from the air; maybe a local town, the coast, or even their house.

Once airborne, if it's safe to do so, let them have a go at controlling the aeroplane under your guidance.

3 TAKE YOUR PARTNER TO ANOTHER AIRFIELD FOR LUNCH

Next step in the process of taking people flying is to plan a trip to another airfield for lunch.

If you have a partner this is a great way to earn some points for all of the time and money spent learning to fly. You can now share the benefits and treat them to a trip away. Pick a sunny day and wow them with the views and your new skills.

If you do it right, you'll be receiving requests to go on flying trips more often as a result!

4 OFFER TO TAKE TRIAL FLIGHTS FOR A FLYING CLUB

Changes in regulations during 2015 have opened up one of the most interesting opportunities for private pilots to fly more often by taking trial flights for flying clubs.

The pilot must be of sufficient experience and capabilities, and must operate within the restrictions of the club's insurance and currency limits. The pilot also must not earn any money for operating these flights (they are not required to pay to fly, either).

This is a great way to build hours and experience. It doesn't offer much freedom in terms of where you get to fly – after all, you are providing a service and an experience for the customers. However, for any pilot struggling to afford to build hours for a commercial career, or interested in gaining a flight instructor rating, this is great way to go about it. Speak to your flying club owner to see if they could offer you any of their trial flights, say on a Saturday or Sunday when they are most busy.

CHAPTER 7

CHEAPER WAYS TO FLY

Flying is not a cheap hobby. It's not even cheap to pursue as a career.

The costs involved are often so much of a hindrance to pilots that they drop away from it, or end up flying very rarely.

In this section I want to offer some tips on how you can save money whilst flying, and take opportunities to avoid wasting money by planning ahead or offering to help others in exchange for flying.

If you can master this and budget effectively, there's no reason for you to have to stop flying or put unacceptable limits on getting airborne.

1 AVOID WASTING MONEY

Let's face it, flying is expensive. So if we can become smarter about what we spend and avoid unnecessary expenses, that's surely a good thing, right?

The main costs of flying are fuel, aircraft hire, training, landing fees and aircraft maintenance (for those lucky enough to own an aircraft).

So I challenge you to plan ahead and be more aware of where costs will occur and do something to reduce or avoid them, to allow you more time in the air and less time wishing you could afford it. Here are some further tips on how to achieve this:

2 GET REQUIRED FLIGHTS DONE IN PLENTY OF TIME

Make sure you book a solo flight in plenty of time to avoid having to do a 28 day check ride with an instructor, especially when the weather is forecast to cause problems. This will save you the extra expense of a dual flight for the sake of flying a solo flight.

3 GET HOLD OF FREE LANDING VOUCHERS

When planning different airfields to visit, make use of free landing vouchers available in magazines, or fly-in events with no landing fees.

Vouchers often have an expiry date, so make sure you visit the airfields in the correct order so as to make use of the free landings.

4 BUY FLYING TIME IN A LUMP SUM

If you have some money to spare and plan to fly fairly often, a good way to save on the cost of each flight is by putting a lump sum into your account at the flying club. This usually leads to a reduction in hire rates, or a free flight now and then.

Ask your flying club if they can offer a discount on training or hire rates if you pay a lump sum up front.

5 SHOP AROUND FOR MAINTENANCE AND OTHER SERVICES

Shop around for your aircraft maintenance, and plan it well in advance to take advantage of the best rates.

Using the same company that you always have is not necessary, and you may find someone at your home airfield or closer, saving on the cost of the expensive ferry flight.

6 CONSIDER SECOND HAND EQUIPMENT

If you need some new equipment check classifieds or online auction listings to see if a cheaper second-hand version is available. Online forums and Facebook groups are another source for second-hand equipment.

7 SET ASIDE MONEY AND BUDGET FOR FLYING

It goes without saying that flying is not the cheapest hobby, and training in particular can take up large chunks of your budget. Whether you're thinking of learning to fly, or already a qualified pilot, no doubt money is an issue which crops up and determines how often you're going to be able to get in the air or take lessons.

Key to being able to fly more is in budgeting for it. Be realistic about what you can afford and when you will have the funds to pay for flying. When I decided to learn to fly, I made the promise to myself that I would not get into debt doing it, but would wait until I had the funds to pay for it entirely. This meant that a lack of money did not hold up my lessons and progress towards getting my licence.

Since then, I've budgeted for a monthly flying allowance to myself. It's never possible to fly as much as I'd like, but at least I rarely have to stop flying completely.

8 FIND LOCAL COMPANIES WHO OFFER CHEAP HOUR-BUILDING PACKAGES

Hour building is something that is important to pilots who want to advance in their training and undertake additional ratings and licences. Everything from flight instructor to commercial airline pilot training have set minimum hours of experience requirements for entry on to the course, often in the multiple hundreds of hours.

Hiring an aircraft from the flying club now and then is not a cost-efficient or easy way to build these required hours. So a good step is to find a cheap hour-building package whereby you have access to an aircraft to fly at a much reduced rate.

Flying clubs usually need their aircraft for lessons and are reluctant to let them go for extended periods at reduced costs, but it's always worth asking. There may be a company who bases aircraft at your local airfield which can offer this service if you ask around. Often aircraft dealers are willing to let you use aircraft that they have for sale instead of leaving them sat on the ground for extended periods.

9 FIND THE CHEAPEST AIRCRAFT TYPES AVAILABLE TO YOU

Just like driving, where we all want to have the best car, it's not always practical, sensible or cost effective to be flying the best aircraft on offer at your flying club. Sometimes, if we want to build hours or fly more often, it makes sense to find the aircraft which is most cost effective to fly.

This is also true when you are looking to buy an aircraft or a share in an aircraft. Think of the running costs or hire costs and how much this will add up to over time to work out whether you can afford to fly as often as you wish.

I chose to learn to fly in a two-seat aircraft, and carried on flying it for many months after gaining my PPL simply because of costs. Then, only when I felt I could justify it, I converted to flying four-seat aircraft. It was a nice treat to do so, and meant I could take more people flying. But I still often went back to the two-seater when it was only me flying.

10 OFFER HELP IN EXCHANGE FOR FLYING TIME

Many a fresh pilot has funded his or her training or aircraft hire charges by working for the flying club. Could you do this and be paid in flying time?

Flying clubs are often run on a shoestring and any additional help will no doubt be gratefully received if you have a good reputation with the owner or manager. You could offer to wash and clean aircraft, refuel aircraft, man the reception desk or process security passes.

Here's another tip – aircraft often need to be taken to another airfield for maintenance or scheduled checks. Could you offer to take the aircraft and sit with it while the work is carried out, then bring it back? It's two free flights, after all!

CHAPTER 8

FLYING ABROAD

From the safety of your home airfield the prospect of taking a trip to another country can be daunting. There are the language barriers, customs regulations, long distances and often seas to cross.

Pushing your comfort zone, however, is part of being a pilot. With proper instruction, advice and preparation, flying aboard need not be different to any other cross-country flight, yet it can open up a world of interesting new experiences.

Then, there are opportunities to base yourself at a foreign airfield to take advantage of better weather, cheaper flying, and new sights to explore.

1 PLAN YOUR FIRST FLIGHT ABROAD

It's a daunting thing to step into the unknown like this. Flying in the UK is a somewhat insular experience for pilots like myself, and it takes a bit of courage to finally leave these shores (perhaps not so much for pilots based on parts of the British south coast, where France is only 25 miles away).

Flying abroad introduces a range of new experiences for pilots, from crossing an extended stretch of water (again, I'm thinking of UK pilots), to customs clearance, different procedures and air traffic control which may not speak perfect English, as well as that daunting 'unknown' any of us feel when flying to a new airfield.

Thankfully in Europe we have commonality across most borders thanks to EASA's standards, and English is widely spoken well at even smaller airfields. So this first step need not be so daunting, and airfields are generally welcoming of foreign light aircraft visiting them.

Remember that crossing borders will often mean arranging customs clearance, and when flying to France don't be too tempted to try the wine if you're flying back the same day!

If you're planning to fly abroad for the first time, speak to other pilots who have done the trip and pick their brains. It might be best to take another pilot along who has done such a trip before to offer advice along the way.

2 JOIN A FLYING HOLIDAY

If you lack the experience or confidence in flying long distances alone, or can't find a pilot to join you, there are flying holidays which any pilot can tag along with.

These trips are usually organised by experienced companies who will do all of the planning and offer a safe, supportive environment for taking a group trip on an adventure overseas or to a different part of the country. It adds a fun social element and gives you experience in navigating over long distances and even formation flying.

Guided tours and air adventure trips can be found in locations such as Australia, Africa, New Zealand, across Europe and the United States. It is often possible to join in as a pilot, or hire aircraft for the trip, if you don't have your own.

3 FLY IN THE USA

America is the largest nation for flying anywhere in the world. There are more private pilots here than anywhere and the world of light sport flying is big business. It is generally cheaper to fly in America, and in many of the states there is a much better weather record than in countries such as the UK and Ireland.

Anyone with a European Private Pilot's Licence can fly in the USA after a filling out a FAA form and taking an hour of instruction with an instructor at a FSDO (a

US flying school with a designated instructor for foreign pilots). Details of these can easily be found online, and are prolific in states such as Florida. Then, with your check ride completed, you can go ahead and hire aircraft to fly in the USA.

Doing so can be a great adventure, with hundreds of small airfields across every state and a great attitude towards recreational flying. Radio communications are generally less rigid than in Europe, and fuel is cheaper.

There are organisations which can arrange flying holidays, or you can do the research yourself. Just make sure you fill out the form in plenty of time to avoid experiencing delays at the start of your trip.

4 FIND A GROUP AND GO ON A LONG TRIP

Do you ever read pilot magazines and that articles about groups of pilots who undertake a really long journey in their light aircraft? Well these kinds of trips are not out of reach and usually just require a bit of planning and logistics to make happen.

In most cases, it stems from a desire to fly to a particular place, or to undertake an adventure unlike any kind of flight taken before.

Researching the route and airports along the way takes a bit of time, thinking through fuel availability, time in the air, distances and any red tape likely to be encountered. Then picking the right time of year is important to maximise the daylight available and minimise the chance of weather cancellations.

Trips over long distances to other countries can often define a flying career for a private pilot, boost confidence and create lasting memories. They should be something all pilots try at least once.

5 EXPLORE FRANCE

Various airfields along the north east coast of France, such as Le Touquet and Calais – Dunkerque, are inundated with British light aircraft throughout the year because they are so close to Britain and make an easy day trip or first flight abroad. It is recommended that any pilot try these as a first step.

Next, with your confidence in flying in these foreign skies growing, why not venture further inland and explore France a little? The country is a very popular place for recreational flying, offering many airfields in some wonderful scenery, including the spectacular *Rhône-Alpes region.*

Finding maps and trip reports from other pilots is easy, and digital navigational software options usually cover France.

6 SPEND TIME FLYING IN FLORIDA

Flying in the USA is mentioned earlier in this chapter as a great challenge and fun experience for pilots. In this section I want to focus specifically on Florida, which is arguably the country's best place to fly.

Many pilots will come to Florida to undertake their entire training, whether for a private licence, or to go all the way to a commercial licence. The reason they do this is for the great weather (nearly every day is a flying day), the cheap prices for training, fuel and aircraft hire, and the proliferation of airports and flying schools.

If you've already got your licence maybe you're just looking for somewhere different to go and fly. There are plenty of airfields with holiday accommodation which backs onto the airfield and your own aircraft to use for exploring the state, and which are close enough to the other tourist attractions to make it fun for regular holiday activities, too.

If you're still thinking of learning to fly, consider Florida from the outset. Often the cost of flights from Europe, accommodation and training can be equivalent to the full licence in Europe, but can be done in a much shorter time and a more pleasant environment. Just remember you'll need to convert your licence once you get back home.

CHAPTER 9

———

GOING ALL THE WAY – AIRLINES AND FLYING CAREERS

f your purpose in learning to fly is to continue all the way to a career flying for airlines or for other commercial purposes, there are steps you can take at each stage of your path as a pilot to ensure you make the most of opportunities to fly more.

At lot of what you can do is in preparing yourself for the road ahead, through exams, ratings, hour building and usually spending a lot of money to get there!

1 DECIDE IF AN AIRLINE CAREER IS REALLY FOR YOU

Have you already got a pilot's licence? You may have that dream of becoming an airline pilot, however until you've had a little experience in flying an aeroplane you should not commit to the huge costs involved until you know it feels right for you.

It's not necessary to have a PPL in order to start training as an airline pilot as some courses and sponsorships take new recruits without any experience.

It is worthwhile checking that you have the correct educational and personal attributes which airlines are looking for, too.

2 READ A BOOK ABOUT THE LIFE OF AN AIRLINE PILOT

We are all partial to dreaming and imagining what life would be like as a commercial airline pilot. We see only the good things as we rarely have first-hand experience.

However, life flying for an airline can be incredibly stressful and involve a lot of pressure and time away from home. Then there are the early morning starts and late finishes.

There are a number of books by airline pilots that explain the job and its ups and downs from a personal perspective. I recommend The Flightdeck Survival Manual by James McBride as an honest account of what it's like to work as an airline pilot.

Maybe you know an airline pilot and could ask them what it's like as a career.

3 MAKE AN HONEST FINANCIAL ASSESSMENT

Learning to fly is very expensive. If you've already gained a PPL you'll know this… but a full Airline Transport Pilot Licence (ATPL) is a whole lot more expensive!

The exact amount depends on whether you complete it in a modular fashion, or an all-in course. Typically you can expect to pay between £60,000 – £120,000 to gain the full licence.

There are of course sponsorships available, and if you've already gained some licences the modular cost will be reduced. It is important at this stage to work out if this kind of financial burden is possible for you, and how you would raise the money and pay it back.

Remember, gaining the licence is only one step towards becoming an airline pilot. Finding the job may not be immediate, and as an entry level First Officer you will not be on the highest wages at first.

4 ATTEND A PILOT TRAINING EVENT

There are regular events held each year to help prospective airline pilots find out more about courses, sponsorships, and the many different aspects involved in training.

If you're serious about becoming an airline pilot, but still a bit lost about how to go about it, attending one of these events is a useful thing to do. You'll be able to speak to many different organisations and airlines in one day and ask any questions you have. It will help you understand the costs, requirements and what's involved.

Pilot Career News put on a number of 'Live' events around Europe each year, including Dublin, Frankfurt, London, Madrid, Leeds and Rome. Find out more at their website **www.pilotcareernews.com/live/**

5 RESEARCH SPONSORSHIP OPPORTUNITIES WITH AIRLINES

Money is naturally one of the biggest hurdles in gaining an airline pilot licence. Depending on how you go about your training, it can cost over £100,000. If you're young, chances are you don't have that kind of money in your back pocket, and most of us don't have a line of rich relatives waiting to give us the money.

One popular means of funding your training is by receiving sponsorship from an airline, whereby they pay your training costs and, once qualified, you get a job with them to pay it back. There is a lot of competition for sponsorships, and the selection process is naturally much

The route to becoming an airline pilot is expensive and difficult, but very rewarding.

more rigorous – you'll need to be confident that you can pass the aptitude tests and impress the selection team, as you're effectively having a job interview for an airline before even starting training.

Every year hundreds of pilots are successful in following this route, however, so why shouldn't it be you?

Do some research today into the sponsorship schemes available. Each airline tends to partner with a particular training company, so you may need to do some searching. For example, British Airways use FTE Jerez, CTC Aviation and CAE Oxford (as do Flybe), easyJet also uses CTC.

6 PLAN EXTRA TRAINING IF YOU'RE ALREADY A PILOT

If you've already got a pilot's licence, then maybe you want to pursue a modular approach to becoming an airline pilot. This can be an easier way of affording the expense of training and completing it when funds allow.

Work out where you're at now, and form a plan to get to the next stage down the line.

For example, do you have a PPL and night rating? A good next step would be to consider adding a Flight Instructor (FI) rating. This will open up opportunities allowing you to build up hours quickly and affordably whilst working for a local flying club and teaching new pilots.

Maybe you're already an instructor and want to take some more steps. How about adding your multi-engine licence or commercial licence? Previously Flight Instructors were required to hold a commercial licence, but this is not the case any longer. However, it is important for airline pilots to have this.

Finally, if you're already more advanced than most and have lots of qualifications and hours under your belt, but not quite enough for taking a step into the airlines, check out jobs with fixed base operators such as executive aircraft operators, medical repatriation companies, parachute companies or even small cargo airlines.

CHAPTER 10

IMPROVE YOUR
FLYING TECHNIQUE

Whether it's days, months or years since you became a pilot, you should never forget your training or stop learning. It's simply too important to avoid making mistakes, becoming a bad pilot, or risking the safety of your aircraft and passengers.

What's more, committing to improving your abilities as a pilot and revisiting what you learned is a sure way to fly more. It could be an excuse to get up and fly a manoeuvre for an hour, or used as preparation for a future flight which you intend to take.

There are many ways to learn as a pilot, from written material to other pilots. Taking instruction on flying is open to any pilot, not just those actively training.

1 REVISIT YOUR TRAINING

How long ago did you train to become a pilot? Do you remember the strain of trying to learn all of the new techniques, studying for the written exams, trying to keep on top of navigation, emergencies, advanced skills?

If it's been more than a year since you gained your licence, chances are you have already put so much of your training to the back of your mind and have no intention of dragging it up again. When was the last time you pulled out your "whizz wheel" before planning a flight?

Forgetting or ignoring your training can have dire consequences and leave you open to bad pilot habits. After all, the foundations we learn in how to fly an aircraft, how to check its airworthiness, how to deal with emergencies, and how to safely plan a flight and navigate are taught for a reason.

So why not take the time to refresh your memory as often as possible? Try and take a particular aspect of flying technique and learn the theory again, or commit to practicing emergency drills and memorising the steps you'd take if it happens in real life. Read through the study books, such as Air Law, Communications, Meteorology and Human Factors and think through their applications to your flying now that you have more hours under your belt.

2 PICK UP SOME GOOD HABITS FROM OTHER PILOTS

Flying alone, or as the only pilot in the plane, is incredibly liberating and fun – a real achievement. But by never flying alongside other pilots you risk developing bad pilot habits and assuming your own knowledge of different situations.

If there is another pilot in the cockpit, situations that arise can be discussed and a best course of action taken. This could be anything from 'Where did the controller tell us to park?' to 'How should we approach this airfield that we've never flown into before?'

It can take a load off your mind in difficult situations, and you can learn a lot from the shared knowledge and experience gained by flying with other pilots.

In addition to this, taking a ride with an instructor should not be shied away from. It can be frustrating to be made to have a check ride after not having flown for a month, or when your biennial anniversary comes around, but I always find I learn something or have a bad habit corrected which is incredibly valuable to my flying. Plus, it's a great opportunity to ask any questions that may have arisen whilst flying, or to catch up on what's new with club aircraft, equipment, airfield procedures etc.

3 READ MAGAZINES ABOUT FLYING

It seems every country has magazines aimed at pilots which cover the whole spectrum from aspiring pilots to those who fly for a living. These monthly publications are a great source of inspiration and usually give ideas on where to fly, and how to get more out of flying. Often they'll include free landing vouchers and plenty of post-mortems on light aircraft incidents and accidents that we can always learn from. And if you're looking to get into aircraft ownership, there are usually classifieds with aircraft for sale, and reviews of new and upcoming aircraft to the market.

4 READ BOOKS ABOUT FLYING

For inspiration and additional instruction on flying, there are many books published each year covering all aspects of being a pilot. Choosing a topic of interest to you, or which you feel is lacking in your own flying skills, and taking the time to drill down into it through a book is a great way of improving your flying (and also of killing time on rainy days).

The fact that you're reading this is hopefully a good indication that you value the inspiration you can find in books. There are also many which offer real-life examples from pilots, at a fraction of the cost of taking a course or hiring an instructor!

A quick scan through a catalogue which arrived through my door recently reveals books on topics such as: test preparation, multi-engine ratings, microlights, meteorology, human performance, aircraft recognition, floatplanes, helicopters, radiotelephony, airline and advanced training, aviation stories and even children's books about flying.

5 PRACTICE YOUR EMERGENCIES

How often have you practiced forced landings after engine failure? In the past year? Or only when you did your training?

What about other emergencies, like radio failure, electrical failure or in-flight fires?

I'm guessing the reason you learned to fly wasn't to spend your hard-earned money training for emergencies when you could be enjoying the scenery and visiting other airfields. But you can only do that if you are fully confident in how to deal with the unexpected situations that can arise any time you fly.

Reading through accident reports which are regularly published in general aviation magazines and online, it's easy to see where things went wrong using the gift of hindsight. However, put yourself in the cockpit with that pilot and take yourself through what they would have been experiencing, or how they got to that point, and think about whether you would have instinctively done things differently, or ended up in the same situation.

Being ready for an emergency could mean the difference between making it back alive and being another article in a magazine dissecting your actions for other pilots to learn from.

Even just going through emergency procedures at home in your mind, with a picture of the cockpit in front of you, is better than never practicing. Commit to doing this a few times per year.

6 IMPROVE YOUR LANDINGS

Landing is a sore point for most pilots. But, as the adage goes, as long as you can walk away from it, it's been a successful one!

Reiterating that point, there's no need to beat yourself up about the occasional bad landing as long as you're not causing undue stress or damage to the aircraft. We can all experience a lack of finesse when there are so many factors thrown into the mix (not least lack of attention or over confidence). However, if this is causing you stress then make a point of working on your landings and revisiting the theory behind the perfect landing.

Some tips I've been told include looking outside, not inside, which can give you a better special awareness ahead of that return to earth. Also getting your speed right on final approach means you're not grappling with the approach, or heading towards a kangaroo jump when the wheels finally hit the floor. If it makes you feel better about flying, this is one to work on.

7 FLY MORE SEAT-OF-YOUR-PANTS

Sometimes flying can be such an overwhelming experience, especially for newer pilots, that to do anything other than flying by the rules, as you've been taught, would be a terrifying prospect likely to end in a mess. Symptoms include gripping the control column, a rigid gaze on the instruments and a permanent frown of concentration.

Flying safely is, of course, the right thing to do. But relax a little – you've overcome your training and been given permission to fly, so go and enjoy it.

Learning to fly by feel and observation is a sign of a comfortable and confident pilot who respects the checklists, but knows instinctively about how to fly. Besides, there's much more to see outside the window than on the instrument panel. So, try looking out there more often! Try to fly by feel when approaching for a landing and learn how the aircraft behaves.

8 FLY LESS SEAT-OF-YOUR-PANTS!

To step back and slightly contradict the previous point, there are pilots out there who disregard rules and wisdom a little too often and ultimately get themselves into trouble.

You may have hundreds of hours on a particular aircraft, but using that as an excuse for disregarding the checklist or flying it beyond the limits it was designed for is never a good idea. Too many accident reports are a result of pilot error where something was forgotten or the aircraft was handled incorrectly.

Enjoy flying, enjoy the view, have fun with the adventure of it all and get good at it. But respect the solemnness of being a pilot; be more Sully than Maverick!

9 GET AN INSTRUCTOR'S CRITIQUE

Most pilots hate this one, but bear with me. Flight instructors are paid to be good enough to teach people to fly, and to spot and correct problems with the flying technique of pilots before they develop into a bad habit. They have committed the theory behind flying to memory and teach it every day.

No matter how many hours you have under your belt, how much extra reading you've done and experience you've gained, it never hurts to have someone critique your flying now and then.

As with driving a car, we truly learn to master the skill once we have passed the test and begun driving on our own. Flying aircraft is the same. Yet bad habits will naturally start to form at this stage, without anyone to correct us, and only our own understanding to rely on. Over time these bad habits are accepted as the correct way of flying.

During further training, your biennial check ride, or simply on a flight which you have arranged with an instructor, ask them to spot any of these bad habits or incorrect ways of flying. Take it on the chin and be ready to accept correction, and even discuss it through if you don't agree.

10 PRACTICE BEING LOST

A pilot is never lost, only "uncertain of position", as we tell ATC. It can happen at any time, particularly when flying across unfamiliar areas, or in marginal weather where visibility is reduced or cloud obscures your view. Most of the time you'll be able to work out your position within a few minutes and continue your flight, and the addition of navigation apps to cockpits has helped things considerably – particularly when it comes to avoiding infringing controlled airspace.

Try not to lose the manual skills in determining your position when lost, and practice this when you fly. The normal flow should be:

Use your map and pick a distinctive landmark which you can see outside the window to determine where you are. Good landmarks include railway intersections, racecourses, castles, cathedrals, motorway junctions and airfields.

If still uncertain, use radio transmissions to ask for guidance from the air traffic service being provided.

Always be aware of your fuel quantities and the minimum safe altitude of the area when uncertain of position, and be prepared to make a precautionary landing if a search proves unfruitful, or if fuel, weather and darkness threaten the safety of the flight.

11 PRACTICE SPINS

Since the PPL syllabus does not require practical training in spins, only theory and written understanding, chances are you have never experienced one. I know many training aircraft are not even certified to undertake them.

Many pilots choose to gain experience in spinning and recovery from spins as a wise safety measure should the ugly situation arise when training. This is entirely up to you; maybe you feel that theory is enough and do not wish to encounter such stomach-churning manoeuvers in real life.

Having the experience in recovering from spins is a valuable skill for pilots, however. Simply recognising the onset of an incipient spin may not be enough if, for whatever reason, it develops fully and leaves you falling from the sky.

Flying schools with instructors and aircraft capable of demonstrating and training in spin recovery are always available to do so. It may just save your life one day.

12 WATCH VIDEOS OF OTHERS FLYING

It has become so easy to record flights with action cameras and smartphones and share them on YouTube and forums for others to enjoy.

I find that I can search for any airfield and there will usually be someone who has filmed the arrival or departure in a light aircraft.

And then there are many pilots who share videos of the full flight, which are great for observing navigation techniques and simply enjoying the view in places you might never have flown.

If you find yourself grounded because of the weather, or planning a trip to an airfield you've never visited before, it can be a valuable and enjoyable exercise to watch videos of others flying for inspiration.

13 GO THROUGH SOME REFRESHER WORK WITH AN INSTRUCTOR

Another rainy-day tip for the times that you're grounded

but want some flying experience. Any instructors who are grounded will be at a loose end when their lessons are cancelled. If you've had a question about an aspect of flying, aircraft management or maintenance, emergency procedures, or anything else that has been puzzling you, they'll probably love the opportunity to sit down with you and talk it through.

Refreshing your knowledge of flying once you have your pilot's licence is not a sign of weakness, but an essential part of keeping safe in the air. It may be years since you last had instruction on flying, but these guys are teaching it every day. So brush up on your knowledge whenever you can!

14 TEST YOUR PILOT KNOWLEDGE

When was the last time you picked up one of the training books you used when taking flying lessons? Could you even remember half of what's in there if you took the test today?

These books, and many more which are available to buy, have practice quizzes to test your understanding of different

subjects. Try a few out and see where the gaps in your knowledge have formed, and plan to get back up to speed by re-reading those chapters and refreshing your memory.

Staying safe in the air is your responsibility. We all must stay on top of that knowledge if we are to perform our flying well and not risk our own safety or that of other pilots and our passengers.

15 TAKE VIDEOS OF YOUR FLYING

As well as watching videos that other pilots have taken on sites such as YouTube, it's also great fun to take videos of your own flights! Portable cameras are available quite cheaply, however the standard seems to be the GoPro, which is known to produce good results and come with a range of attachments for aircraft cockpits and exteriors.

For ideas on where to attach cameras in the cockpit, or on how to wire up to record air traffic control transmissions, there are numerous articles available online.

Recording your flights is a great way to keep lasting memories of the places you visit and the sights you see from the air. You can either fix the camera into one all-encompassing viewing position, or move it around during flights. Those of you with extra deep pockets could even fix multiple cameras throughout the cockpit or on the wings (note, attaching peripherals to the exterior of an aircraft needs to be done within the operating guidelines for that aircraft).

Having videos of your flight is also a good way to gain feedback on your flying techniques. For example, if you're going through a spell of bad landings, watching playback of your flights can offer an insight into what you might be doing wrong. You could even show an instructor or another pilot to get their input.

CHAPTER 11

OLD DOG? WAYS TO KEEP FLYING

Thissection is aimed squarely at pilots who have been around the circuit pattern a few times.

The heady days of youth when the pilot's licence was fresh and the opportunities seemed limitless are long behind you and it's sometimes difficult to find inspiration to keep it valid.

These tips hopefully offer some inspiration to get you flying again, and ways you might reignite that interest.

1 GET FLYING AGAIN

If you haven't used your pilot's licence in a while, often the biggest factor stopping you is a lack of motivation or confidence. You could have hundreds of hours, and many years' experience under your belt, but if it has been a while you just don't feel up to getting in the cockpit.

The most important thing is to just do it; get flying again, and realise why you used to love it and why you got the licence in the first place.

If it has been a long time, you will need to ensure that your licence is still valid. Not having a revalidation flight every two years means you'll need to take a check ride with an instructor and reactivate your licence. However, taking some refresher flights with an instructor is advisable anyway after long periods without flying, to give you the confidence of having someone in the cockpit next to you, and to go over any areas that have become a little rusty.

2 MAKE A BUCKET LIST (WHAT HAVEN'T I ACHIEVED IN FLYING?)

If you're stuck in a rut with your flying and feel disenchanted by continuing to do the same thing every time you fly, you're probably not likely to keep it up much longer. So maybe it's time to take stock and think back to when you first learned to fly.

Why did you gain a licence? What did you want to do with it? Where did you want to fly? How far did you want to take it?

If you haven't achieved any of these ambitions yet, ask yourself if you would still like to do them. It's the perfect time to make a bucket list.

3 MAKE A BUCKET LIST OF AIRCRAFT TYPES

Maybe it's time to explore new aircraft types. If you've got the experience, you shouldn't need too much instruction to convert to a new type, even if it's just for a few hours of fun and not necessarily for the long haul.

Are there any historic aircraft, such as the Tiger Moth, which you'd like to fly? Or maybe a microlight or brand new touring aircraft.

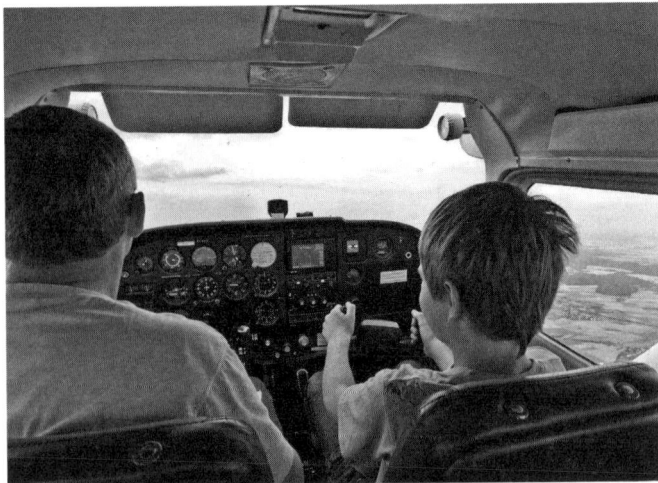

Passing on your knowledge to the next generation of pilots can be incredibly rewarding.

4 MAKE A BUCKET LIST OF DESTINATIONS

Flying is about going places, so where do you still want to go? Do you want to explore a particular part of the country, or even fly abroad? Are there airfields you haven't visited in a long time, or ones which have changed since you last visit (the lure of a good bacon sandwich is enough for most pilots). Make a list of destinations you want to fly to and plan to tick them off.

5 TAKE A YOUNG PILOT UNDER YOUR WINGS

If you've been flying for a lot of years then chances are it's something you value in your life and would recommend to others. Therefore, why not give something back and take a young pilot under your wings.

Even if you're not a flying instructor, it can be very rewarding to encourage someone who has shown interest in flying by taking them for a flight, letting them take control of the plane, and talking them through the process to help their understanding. Having that experience may be the catalyst to set them off on a flying career, and being a mentor to them could make it a little easier for them to make progress, and give you an excuse to fly a little more.

6 JOIN AOPA

The Aircraft Owners and Pilots Association is the largest membership of private pilots in the world, and incredibly influential in promoting and advocating pilots and aircraft owners. It has national outlets around the world, such as AOPA UK.

Becoming a member of AOPA has many benefits for a private pilot, including advice and support when threatened with legal action, incentives for further flight training, and mentoring schemes for advancing beyond the standard licences, such as their Wings Award Scheme. AOPA also publishes its own GA Magazine and other print and online publications which can help pilots with technical knowledge and inspiration for getting more out of flying.

To find out more or join AOPA, visit **www.aopa.co.uk** (UK pilots), or **www.aopa.org** (US pilots).

CHAPTER 12

HAVE A SUCCESSFUL FLIGHT

Most pilots would admit there are gaps in their knowledge or aspects of flying which just aren't perfect. It's easy to get away with most things or settle for how you've always done it, but there's no reason not to make a commitment to learn some good practices to combat those problem areas and improve the way you fly.

Some of the most important aspects of getting the most out of flying come from not being a hero. Knowing your limits, preparing properly, looking after yourself and planning flights thoroughly ensure you not only get your wheels back on earth safely every time, but also enjoy the experience along the way.

1 LEARN TO BE FLEXIBLE

Too many pilots have come to grief by not being flexible and pushing to start or continue a flight when it is simply not safe to do so. Few will get away with being a hero too many times, and it pays to give yourself the option to say No to a flight and reschedule.

Therefore, when planning to fly, be ready from the outset to either change your time or day of departure if factors such as weather, aircraft serviceability, or even your own health don't live up to the standards you require when the time arrives. Often pilots will feel pressure if they are up against a deadline, or if they have promised to fly passengers at a particular time and would rather take the risk instead of letting them down.

2 PLAN AHEAD

Learning to prepare for your flights is an important step in becoming a safer and more proficient pilot, and in ensuring your aerial adventures go as planned.

Being rushed with every flight, or not having a plan for the route or the weather leaves you prone to being caught out or making mistakes once in the air, and ultimately experiencing an unsafe and unenjoyable flight.

Using Notices to Airmen (NOTAMs) and properly checking weather forecasts can save you a lot of problems later.

3 BE PHYSICALLY PREPARED

Making sure you have a great night's sleep and eat well before a flight can be one of the most important ways to fly more safely.

Climbing into the cockpit when you're tired, weak from hunger, stressed from being busy, or not in the best health can lead to serious problems once in the air. In my own experience, I once flew after missing lunch and experienced a terrifying moment when my blood sugar clearly hit a low point and I began to feel shaky and had a buzzing in my ears. It was difficult to focus, and I found myself wondering whether I needed to pick a field and hope for the best, or whether I could teach my passenger to fly in the next few seconds! It's really not worth the risk.

4 MENTALLY REHEARSE THE FLIGHT

That includes the route, landmarks and no-fly zones (particularly in VFR), radio frequency changes, and the layout of the destination airfield. What will happen at each stage in the flight, and what will you need to do?

If this will be a training or renewal flight, mentally prepare for what you will be tested on and rehearse how to perform the manoeuvres, emergencies, checklists and questions you may be asked.

One of the most confident I've ever felt flying was when I had made the time to go through everything I'd have to demonstrate on a biennial check ride and talked through it out loud. I then repeated the process and had a very enjoyable flight which went very smoothly.

Compare that with the time I was running late at the office and dashed to the airport for a check ride without any preparation and expecting to get through it quickly. In reality I was flustered, forgetful, at risk of letting the plane get ahead of me, particularly on final approach, and just didn't enjoy the experience.

5 DON'T RISK IT IN ADVERSE CONDITIONS

Weather is the cause of too many aviation accidents. Know your limits, and be ready to say No when it is marginal and you're not comfortable with how it might deteriorate.

Check en route and destination forecasts and make sure your flight path gives sufficient height clearance. Come up

with a plan for diversions if the weather does deteriorate (and check the diversion airport forecast too!).

6 GET AHEAD OF THE PLANE WHILST STILL ON THE GROUND

This is a favourite tip of mine, ever since my seat chose to slide back just as I rotated the aircraft off the runway during take-off.

Make sure you set up the cockpit and your seating position well before even thinking of starting the engine. Input radio frequencies in advance, and note down alternatives on your kneeboard.

If using a navigation app or GPS, set up your route and check it is correct. Note down the route and other information on a log sheet on your kneeboard so that you have all of your information handy instantly should you need to find it. It's also worth marking your route on a paper map as a backup should batteries fail!

7 STAY ALERT DURING FLIGHT

Nobody wants to dwell on the worst happening, but it's wise to use your time in-flight to stay alert and be ready for action.

Monitor your flight instruments, particularly engine and oil gauges, fuel tanks and flow, and perform FREDA (Fuel, Radio, Engine, Direction and Altimeters) checks regularly to keep on top of the state of the aircraft.

Make sure you monitor the correct radio frequency, and know your position (whether on a map or GPS) clearly so that any deviations don't catch you by surprise or lead to a loss of situational awareness.

8 STAY AHEAD

As well as staying alert, time en route can be used wisely to prepare for the next steps in the flight. Know what your next heading will be after reaching your upcoming waypoint. Input the next radio frequency into the standby channel if your radio has two channels.

Make a plan of when you will next perform checks, when you will switch fuel tanks, when you will begin your descent and when you need to look out for a landmark or high ground. Doing this ensures that there is no confusion about what comes next, which can be fatal when entering busy airspace or being uncertain of position in an unfamiliar area.

9 PLAN YOUR ARRIVAL BEFORE YOU TAKE OFF

It can be overwhelming when flying to a new airfield that you're not familiar with. Most will have specific instructions on how to join (overhead or straight into the circuit), which direction to fly circuits, which villages to avoid overflying, and obstacles that could cause a problem. These can all be found on airfield charts, and usually on the airfield's website or by speaking to them on the phone.

Before taking off, get the latest charts for the airfield and rehearse in your head the way you'll arrive and what calls you'll need to make on the radio. Use an online satellite map like Google Earth to see what villages and other local landmarks look like from the air, and make notes on your map or kneeboard to keep handy when you do arrive.

10 KNOW YOUR PERSONAL LIMITS AND STICK TO THEM

Let's face it, many are drawn to flying because they love machines, fast jets and just because it's "cool". Top Gun and Tom Cruise have a lot to answer for.

But the best pilots have a deep sense of being conservative in what they should be doing when in control of an aircraft, or when planning to fly.

Knowing your personal limits and sticking to them no matter what external pressures are placed on you is a great habit to have as a pilot. Too many pilots have tried to be heroes and had misadventures after not respecting the limits of their skills and training when it comes to weather, flying unfamiliar aircraft, or flying to unfamiliar destinations.

Coming up with your personal limits is exactly that – personal. Some take the rules about weather minima and the condition of the aircraft instilled into them during training as not to be broken, and that's fine. After all, these are the rules deemed safe by the aviation authority and the aircraft manufacturers.

Others, however, decide on limits based on their experience. You'll often hear of pilots who have landed in winds well above the crosswind limits of their aircraft and feel comfortable doing so because they know how the aircraft behaves and that they have the experience in how to fly it. The same may go for marginal VFR conditions – some pilots would take it as a sign to stay in bed, whilst others are not fazed by the prospect of low cloud and reduced visibility.

Whatever your limits, know them and stick to them. Don't try to be a hero.

11 REHEARSE YOUR CHECKLISTS

That little flipbook checklist, or the laminated card, comes out before every flight (or at least, they should!). Depending on what kind of pilot you are, you'll either skim over it or triple-check every point in detail. Then you'll place it back in your kneeboard and you'll fly.

A little challenge I want to give you is to rehearse the checklist. This does two things – it gets you more familiar with the cockpit, and it forces you to think about what you're checking.

For a long time I followed the points on the checklist and never really thought about what I was checking for. Thankfully things rarely showed signs of a problem, so I didn't have to think through a solution (or cancelling the flight).

Rehearsing your checklists at home with a picture of the cockpit you fly in takes your thought process through the checks and what it means to the safety of the flight. You're not up against any pressure to get airborne from another aircraft waiting behind you, or because ATC are pushing to slot you in amongst the traffic.

Once it's committed to memory you'll be a more efficient pilot and hopefully safer at spotting and dealing with issues should they ever arise.

CHAPTER 13

———

LOOKING AFTER YOUR PLANE

W hether you own a plane outright, own a share in one, or simply hire aircraft from a flying club when needed, we all have a responsibility to look after it in a way that ensures its continued airworthiness and safety for pilots.

Unlike cars, aeroplanes have more stringent guidelines on inspections and certification which occur more frequently than a standard MOT or service. Similarly, it's important to be aware of the extra stresses placed on an airframe during flight and the need to always be able to return it safely to the ground.

This section explores the ways we can look after our aircraft properly to ensure we are able to fly when we want to.

1 BEFORE YOU FLY

The moments before taking an aircraft into the air are arguably the most important in ensuring you have a safe and successful flight. This is the chance to make sure everything is in order to enable you to safely and legally fly.

Before you even leave the flying club or home there are items for you to check, such as the technical log of the aircraft which shows the recent flights it has taken, any technical issues noted by other pilots, and the amount of fuel it should have inside its tanks. At this point you should also check that the aircraft has enough hours left to fly before it is due its next inspection or annual check.

There should be a logbook for your aircraft which includes its certificate of registration, permit to fly, aircraft radio licence, and logbooks of work carried out. (Some of these documents need to be carried on board the aircraft if you are flying internationally).

Assuming all is well, out at the aircraft you have checklists for ensuring the aircraft is in a fit state to fly. I do not need to take you through these, but stress the need to perform particularly thorough checks if this is the aircraft's first flight of the day (or even longer), testing every system and checking the engine, fuel and oil.

2 AFTER YOU FLY

After landing, with the aircraft parked up, checklists completed and passengers safely extracted ready for the obligatory group photograph, there are a few considerations you should take.

First of all, will this be the final flight of the day for this aircraft? If so, it is your job to secure it for the night by tying down if possible, putting chocks in front of the wheels, and leaving the cockpit in a presentable way with all systems turned off. If wind is forecast many pilots choose to angle the aircraft nose into the anticipated wind direction, to place additional ties to the ground, and also to link the seatbelts around the control columns, which have been pulled back.

Finally, make a quick inspection of the aircraft to check for any damage which may have come from the flight and be ready to make a note in the logbook of your flying times, tachometer and fuel use.

3 WEATHER CONSIDERATIONS

The kinds of weather you fly in are dictated by the rules of your licence, for example visual flight rules (VFR) or instrument flight rules (IFR), and also to some extent by your own personal limits which have been gained through experience.

There are also weather considerations which pertain to the protection of your aircraft.

As mentioned previously, wind is a serious factor for aircraft on the ground. If not tied down properly, strong winds can easily flip an aircraft onto its back or into other aircraft causing irreparable damage. Tie-downs can be purchased to ensure aircraft are secure during high winds (and should be used overnight regardless of forecasted conditions as an extra safety measure). Many airports and airfields provide these for light aircraft.

Every pilot has their own preferred knot for tying down aircraft, and a couple of them should suffice to hold it. Just remember not to tie the rope completely taut; leave a little room for the wings to move and flex, just not enough to pick up any momentum. And remember the next pilot who will have to untie your knot!

Another weather consideration is rain. Ensuring your aircraft is as watertight as possible will protect the interior, electrics and engine from water damage. Make sure the window and luggage hatches are locked shut, and that the doors are properly closed and sealed. If your aircraft has a cover, place it on securely.

Accumulations of ice on wings can be fatal for flying.
Make sure it is removed safely and completely.

Finally, ice is a problem encountered in many parts of the world during winter. Pilots should be acutely aware of the dangers it poses to aircraft in the air. However, on the ground there are considerations for removing it safely so as not to damage the aircraft. Using a rubber scraper is a safe way to remove ice from wings, and should not damage the metal or remove paintwork like plastic and metal scrapers. If using de-icing fluid, remember to use approved products, such as glycol, which is a Type III substance suitable for use on slower-moving aircraft. Make sure the fluid does not enter any areas not suitable for them, such as the fuel tanks, engine or even the cabin!

When keeping an aircraft at an airport where extremes of weather are regularly experienced, the best way possible to ensure its safety is by keeping it inside a hangar. This is not always possible due to the expense of doing so, or a lack of available space.

4 BUY THE RIGHT EQUIPMENT

It goes without saying that cutting corners when it comes to aircraft safety does not work well. If you own or regularly use an aeroplane, it makes good sense to use equipment and products which are approved for it, so as not to damage the aircraft.

This goes for critical items for flight, such as using the correct grade of oil, as well as de-icing fluids and other lubricants.

It also goes for the many peripheral items pilots choose to add to their flying, such as camera mounts in the cabin and on the airframe, decals, headsets and extra instruments.

Check with the manufacturers, or with other pilots, before committing to buying equipment to make sure it is compatible and safe for your aircraft.

CHAPTER 14

WHAT TO DO NEXT

We come to the end of this book and hopefully it has highlighted at least some inspiration and ideas on how to progress with your flying, whether you're a new or seasoned pilot.

The final tip I'd like to offer is on how to deal with the information you have read. There will be some tips which are more relevant or interesting to you than others, and it is not advisable to try and tackle them all at once.

Make a list of the tips you'd like to try out (or mark them in the column if you're reading the print book) and decide on a logical way to do so.

Perhaps there are a few ideas on flying trips that you'd like to do. Group these and decide in which order to try them. Flying to another airfield should obviously come before flying abroad, for example.

Maybe you've decided to add some more ratings to your licence. There is a natural progression through these, so tackle them in the logical order and one at a time so as not to overload yourself.

You could also group tips into times of the year. For example, taking a night rating is only really possible in the winter months, whereas trying to fit lots of airfields into one day is much easier to do in the longer summer days.

I hope this book does prove useful to your flying. Remember it is always there as a reference, and particularly useful when you're grounded due to weather!

Come back to it from time to time and see where you'd like to go with your flying, especially if you feel you're in a rut or haven't made use of your licence to fly nearly as much as you'd hoped you would.

Stay safe and keep flying!

ABOUT THE AUTHOR

Matt Falcus is a private pilot, aviation writer and editor at **DigitalPilotSchool.com**. He has encountered all of the frustrations and joys of flying, and sought ways to experience more of this hobby which has become a real passion.

Based in the north east of England, his flying has slowly been venturing further afield and seen a number of more adventurous and interesting aircraft types added to the single-engine Pipers that he is so used to.

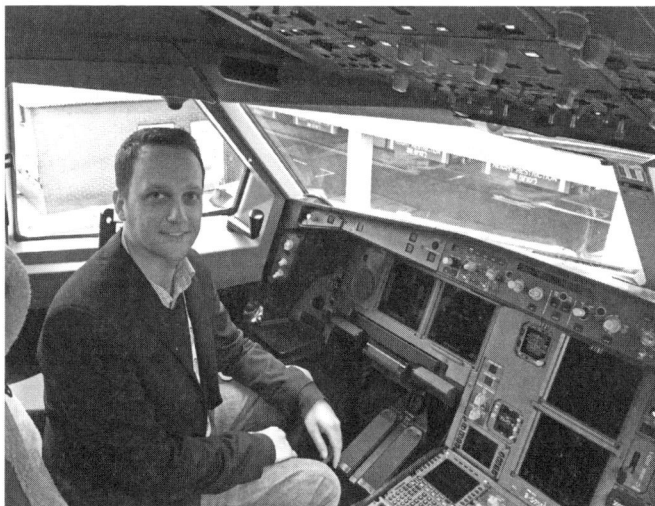

FURTHER READING

TAKE YOUR WINGS AND FLY
A JOURNEY THROUGH A PRIVATE PILOT'S LICENCE
ISBN 978-0-9567187-5-4

Jason Smart, like many people, went through the range of emotions when he set out to learn to fly. In this book, he takes the reader on a journey through the highs and lows of learning to fly, from the early lessons to the first solo, the exams, and ultimately gaining his wings as a private pilot.

In this honest day-by-day account, Jason recounts frustration with the weather, the exhaustion, he encountered and his own limitations, as well as the many characters he meets along the journey.

It also celebrates the feeling of achieving the goal, and being granted wings to fly. It culminates with accounts of Jason's first forays into cross-country trips to a number of airfields.

This book is aimed at anyone interested in learning to fly, or currently training. It is also for anyone simply curious to know what is involved in becoming a pilot.

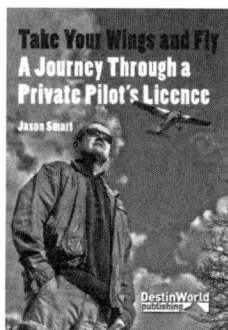

AVAILABLE FROM AMAZON AND
WWW.DESTINWORLD.COM

DIGITAL PILOT SCHOOL

Digital Pilot School – the place with simple tips, advice, resources and inspiration for those who love to fly aircraft.

This website is not only for those learning to fly, but those who have gained their PPL or equivalent licence and want to make the most of opportunities to continue learning and flying. Be it through additional licences, a path to commercial flying, getting into aircraft ownership, or simply looking for inspiration on how to keep on top of your knowledge.

With regular articles and inspiration, and a free email newsletter, visit Digital Pilot School today and become a better pilot.

www.digitalpilotschool.com